Home Office Research Study 233

# Can mentors help primary school children with behaviour problems?

## Final report of the three-year evaluation of Project CHANCE carried out by the Thomas Coram Research Unit between March 1997 and 2000.

Ian St James-Roberts, PhD and Clifford Samlal Singh
Thomas Coram Research Unit, Institute of Education, University of London

*The views expressed in this report are those of the authors, not necessarily those of the Home Office (nor do they reflect Government policy).*

Home Office Research, Development and Statistics Directorate
November 2001

# Home Office Research Studies

The Home Office Research Studies are reports on research undertaken by or on behalf of the Home Office. They cover the range of subjects for which the Home Secretary has responsibility. Other publications produced by the Research, Development and Statistics Directorate include Findings, Statistical Bulletins and Statistical Papers.

## The Research, Development and Statistics Directorate

RDS is part of the Home Office. The Home Office's purpose is to build a safe, just and tolerant society in which the rights and responsibilities of individuals, families and communities are properly balanced and the protection and security of the public are maintained.

RDS is also part of National Statistics (NS). One of the aims of NS is to inform Parliament and the citizen about the state of the nation and provide a window on the work and performance of government, allowing the impact of government policies and actions to be assessed.

Therefore –

Research Development and Statistics Directorate exists to improve policy making, decision taking and practice in support of the Home Office purpose and aims, to provide the public and Parliament with information necessary for informed debate and to publish information for future use.

First published 2001

ISBN 1 84082 769.6
ISSN 0072 6435

# Acknowledgements

Evaluation can only work if the project being evaluated is open and responsive to the queries which are raised. We would like to express our appreciation of the outstandingly receptive and thoughtful approach to the evaluation adopted by the CHANCE project team and management committee. Particular thanks are due to the children, families and schools who put time and effort into providing the information needed for the evaluation. Nicola Rotton and Jane Davies assisted with data collection and processing and we have benefited greatly from their help and ideas.

This evaluation was funded by the Home Office Programme Development Unit. We are very grateful to Christine Lehman and Lorna Smith for their guidance and support.

# Foreword

This paper is one of a group of development reports about projects funded by the Home Office Programme Development Unit (PDU), part of the Research Development and Statistics Directorate. The Programme Development Unit existed from 1992 to 2000; it was set up specifically to encourage, fund and develop innovative local projects about issues related to crime and criminal justice. The Unit's objective was to try to build a bridge between pure research and practice. Two cycles of funding were made available: 1992 – 1995 and 1996 – 1999.

Evaluation reports for the five projects in the second phase[1] including this one, are being published in the HORS series. Also being published to coincide with these reports are a small number of evaluation reports[2] from the first phase of the work, which involved extremely experimental approaches both to development and to evaluation. These are being published as Occasional Papers.

All of these reports relate to early intervention initiatives directed at providing support to children who are, as a rule, not offenders but whose lives include a number of the circumstances which have been identified as risk factors for offending. Interventions range from work with young primary school children to initiatives with excluded secondary school pupils and with first time offenders.

The PDU programme was extremely developmental and evaluators were specifically tasked to consider not only the outcomes of the projects (which in many cases, because of the nature of the interventions and the ages of the participants, can only be early or intermediate outcomes), but also to look carefully at the process of development and implementation and to include a substantial core of descriptive material about the participants and their circumstances. The reports provide a great deal of useful material about the characteristics of the young people involved and their families. They also describe the ways in which agencies responsible for interventions relate to their clients and to each other; discuss the practicality and success of interventions themselves and analyse early indicators of success or failure. All of this knowledge is especially relevant to the many new initiatives either under way or planned,

1 Milton Keynes Youth Crime Reduction Project
Meeting Need and Challenging Crime in Partnership with Schools
Dalston Youth Project
Empowering Young People in Rural Suffolk
2 The Dorset Healthy Alliance Project
The Sheffield C'Mon Everybody Project

including the Children and Young Persons' Unit programmes and New Deal for Communities, together with much other national and local crime reduction work. Although the degree of evaluative rigour varies, these reports nonetheless contain valuable and constructive learning about why, for whom, and how intervention should be planned.

Project CHANCE was one of two mentoring projects supported by the Programme Development Unit, the other being the Dalston Youth Project. CHANCE was extremely innovative both in its application of mentoring as an intervention with primary school-aged children and in its development of "solution-focused" mentoring.

This evaluation report contains very positive assessments of the project's implementation, management and professional development. It also notes that the children and their families trusted and valued their mentors highly. However, the findings on outcomes are not consistently favourable. Children, parents and mentors reported positive increases in confidence, self-control and relationships. But, more rigorous standardised assessments of behaviour and school-related measures show improvements only equivalent to those of a comparison group of non-mentored children.

Project CHANCE continued to flourish after the PDU-funded period ended. It has successfully attracted funding from charitable and mainstream sources and has expanded to serve schools in Hackney and Haringey as well as in Islington. The solution-focused model of mentoring is well developed and in 2001, CHANCE worked with up to 120 children.

This report contains useful lessons for those wishing to develop mentoring programmes. Beyond these – or perhaps preceding them – the report also emphasises the need for careful consideration of fundamental questions: what changes are hoped for as a result of mentoring; how and why will mentoring enable these changes, and how will they be measured; how long should mentoring relationships last; and can mentoring be effective as a single intervention, or should it form part of a multi-faceted programme of support. Similar questions are raised in the report of the Dalston Youth Project.[3]

Mentoring is used increasingly frequently either alone or as a component of other interventions. As evaluated evidence from this range of initiatives emerges, it should be possible to identify more clearly what the scope and purpose of mentoring needs to be to achieve particular objectives and to ensure that it is used more thoughtfully and purposively than is always the case at present.

Christine Lehman RDS

3 Clarke & Tarling (2001) An evaluation of the Dalston Youth Project Part II. HORS 232, London, Home Office

# Contents

# Executive summary

Project CHANCE, the subject of this report, is a community-based intervention programme designed to prevent long-term antisocial behaviour, social exclusion and criminal offending.

The project's main programme provides trained mentors who work one-to-one with primary school-aged children who exhibit behaviour problems and other risk factors. The goal is to intervene early, to support and redirect the children away from more serious and long-term problems.

CHANCE was set up in 1996, with funding from the Home Office Programme Development Unit, The National Lottery, and The Cass Foundation.

This report provides a summative evaluation of its progress during the three-year period from March 1997 to March 2000. CHANCE (UK) has continued to develop since that time, and the findings contained in this report have contributed to its development.

The report's aims are to document the evaluation's findings and to identify the resulting lessons for mentor projects and evaluations, as a whole, in this area.

## Main findings

- By targeting primary school-aged children, the project offers a potentially cost-effective, preventive intervention which catches problems before they become entrenched. Teachers are able to identify such children, while children of this age are probably more open to adult influence than they will be as adolescents.
- The project is well managed and considered professional in approach by its stakeholders, including the families, teachers and head teachers who have invested in it. It has kept within its budgets, developed an effective business plan, and succeeded in obtaining funding for extension and expansion.
- The use of mentors to support primary school-aged children with behaviour problems is innovative and the programme has plausible, evidence-based approaches. The first goal is to establish a trusting relationship. The mentor then

builds on this to deliver a solution-focused intervention, designed to increase the child's competencies and resiliency.

- There is clear evidence that the first of the mentors' goals, the building of trusting relationships, is being achieved. The children and their families trust and value the mentors highly.

- The children, their parents and the mentors all report improvements in the children after the mentoring period. The main gains reported are in the development of confidence, self-control and social awareness and relationships.

- Standardised measures of behaviour, school attendance and exclusion, and academic performance were used to assess whether the gains identified at home generalised to the school environment. A comparison group, of children with comparable behaviour problems but without mentors, was assessed in the same way. The mentored children improved in their behaviour, but equivalent improvements were found in the comparison children. Both groups continued to show serious problems.

- This finding may indicate that mentoring cannot achieve significant generalised behavioural change in such children within a year, implying a need for additional supports. It is equally possible that it indicates the need to further develop the solution-focused stage of mentoring.

- During its second and third years of funding, Project CHANCE piloted parent-support and child-peer schemes and pursued continuation funding, as well as running its child-mentor programme.

- These goals were achieved and financial support ensured, but the additional commitments over-extended the project. Fewer children than planned completed the mentor programme, with the result that it proved substantially more expensive than budgeted for. Numbers are currently returning to target levels.

## Questions and lessons raised by the findings

- In three years, CHANCE implemented an outstandingly well-managed mentor programme and achieved many of its goals. The solution-focused stage of mentoring is among its most innovative features and needs further development by CHANCE and other programmes.

- If mentors are to target changes in children's competencies and behaviour, a more specific theory of change is needed to give mentors concrete guidance in how to identify the competencies and enable change.

- Since children's behaviour may improve as they get older, mentors need to be able to identify when an improvement is significant. Benchmarks to identify significant progress in competencies and behaviour need to be developed, calling for collaborations between projects and evaluators.

- The period of a year for mentoring is shorter than some other projects and may be insufficient for such disadvantaged and challenging children. The dosage of mentoring needs to be reviewed alongside its theory of change.

- There is evidence that multiple interventions, which target both child competencies and environmental supports, may be most effective in helping children to change. CHANCE has piloted parent-support and child-peer schemes. Combining these with the child-mentor programme, and building closer partnerships between mentors and schools, is likely to prove fruitful.

- The findings strongly emphasise the need for research designs which include comparison groups of children, together with baseline and outcome measures of behaviour, as well as the reports of stakeholders.

- Three-year funding leads projects to seek continuation funding during years two and three, which interferes with the project's implementation. Alternative ways of funding and supporting development projects need to be tried out.

# 1 Background and aims of this evaluation

## Background

In 1997, 4.5 million criminal offences were recorded by the police in England and Wales [Barclay & Tavares 1999]. While the sheer number of these crimes is disturbing and costly for our society, it is the increase over time which is, arguably, the greatest source of concern. Since the 1920s, recorded crime has increased by 5 per cent, on average, each year [Barclay & Tavares 1999]. This suggests both that our crime rate has mirrored our society's development and, more optimistically, that it might be possible to prevent many of the crimes if the underlying social processes can be understood.

Two sorts of research have begun to bear on this issue. Firstly, longitudinal studies have identified many of the social risk factors which increase the likelihood of crime [Farrington 1996; Loeber 1990]. These include both person-centred characteristics, such as childhood hyperactivity and behaviour problems, and environmental factors, such as poverty and poor housing, poor parenting, school exclusion and association with delinquent peers. Of particular importance here is that these risk factors can often be identified in early childhood, before the age of ten years used to define the onset of criminal responsibility [Babinski, Hartsough & Lambert 1999].

Secondly, intervention studies which deliver preventive programmes to individuals who show these risk factors have demonstrated that it is sometimes possible to 'turn them around' [Weissberg & Greenberg 1998]. Much remains to be learned about the generalisability, long-term effectiveness and costs of these programmes, but they provide practical benefits, confirmation of the theory, and a basis for hope.

Project CHANCE, the subject of this report, is a preventive intervention programme of this type. Details will be given later, but the core of the project is to provide trained mentors who work on a one-to-one basis with primary school-aged children who exhibit behaviour problems and other risk factors. The goal is to intervene before problems become entrenched, to support and redirect the children away from long-term antisocial behaviour, social exclusion and criminal offending. The effectiveness, and cost-effectiveness, of this intervention are the subjects of this report.

Project CHANCE was set up as a development project in 1996, with funding from the Home Office Programme Development Unit, the National Lottery Charities Board and the Cass Foundation. This report is the result of a three year evaluation of the project from March 1st 1997, which was funded by The Home Office Programme Development Unit.

## Aims of the evaluation

Because evaluation is a relatively new methodological discipline, it is important to make the aims and scope of this evaluation clear at the outset.

The metaphor underlying evaluation is a developmental one. The aim is not to provide evidence about the effectiveness of an intervention programme after it is over, so much as to support it and assist it in its development. This contrasts with traditional experimental methodologies, where researchers stand back from a treatment trial and provide their findings only after the trial is finished. The evidence from such trials then adds to knowledge, but is too late to be of any use to the intervention programme being assessed. Except in rare cases where the findings can be directly applied to practice, a new trial is required to take the results and issues raised further. This is a potentially slow and wasteful way to make progress. If an intervention project has sufficient resiliency and strength, it may be more efficient to improve it than start over.

In keeping with these principles, our aim in carrying out this evaluation has been to remain intellectually and financially independent of Project CHANCE, but not to stand back from the project or report on it retrospectively. Instead, we have fed back information throughout the three years of the evaluation, to assist the project in developing and reaching its goals. This is sometimes referred to as formative evaluation. This final report provides a summative evaluation, in the sense that it reviews the findings and lessons learned over the three-year evaluation period as a whole. This does not mean that the findings sum up Project CHANCE, since it is continuing to develop. Rather, this report's objective is to review the major lessons learned so far, so that these can be built upon by mentor projects and evaluations in this area in future.

More specifically, this report has the following goals:

1. To describe project CHANCE's main features, rationales and aims during this period
2. To evaluate its effectiveness in implementing its aims
3. To assess the project's immediate outcomes, by measuring the nature and degree of any changes in the children which resulted from having a mentor
4. To evaluate the cost of CHANCE
5. To identify lessons which may help mentor projects and evaluations in this area in general to develop evidence-based policies and practices.

# 2 Project CHANCE's features, aims and rationales

In 1995, David Conroy put forward a proposal to set up Project CHANCE to the Home Office Programme Development Unit under its Reducing Criminality Initiative. The proposal drew on two main sources. '10 Case Studies of Young Offenders', prepared by Islington Police Officers, and Elizabeth Howell's and colleagues' 1994 report 'Vulnerable Young People in Islington' prepared for the Metropolitan Police Community Affairs Branch. The 'Case Studies' drew attention to what has since become firmly established: that many of the most persistent youth offenders in Islington were known to the local police long before they reached criminal age. It recommended trying to intervene preventively, before they embarked fully on a criminal career.

The Howell et al report, too, recommended the introduction of a community-based intervention programme for vulnerable young people in Islington. It used the word 'volunteer' to describe the agent of the programme and suggested an approach which provided support for needy parents and families, rather than one built specifically around the relationship between a mentor and child.

In its proposed form, project CHANCE was intended to have three inter-dependent elements: the primary, child mentor, programme; a parent-support scheme; and a child peer-group scheme. In practice, although both the parent- and peer-group schemes have been piloted, CHANCE has concentrated its resources chiefly on its child mentor programme. Accordingly, we will report briefly on the two subsidiary schemes later in this report, but will focus mainly on the child mentor programme.

CHANCE began in 1996 and had settled into a more or less stable form when our evaluation began in March 1997. The project team included a full-time co-ordinator, two full-time programme support workers and a part-time administrator. This team was supported by a management committee, which included senior representatives from local education, police, health, and schools. CHANCE was, and is, located in offices in Islington in central London.

The CHANCE child mentor programme was designed to be delivered to around 40 children per year. It included several innovative and appealing features:

## Targeting children in the primary school age-range.

As noted earlier, it is possible to identify child and environmental risk factors which predict later criminal offending by this age. It is known, too, that juvenile offenders commit a disproportionate number of crimes, that they are particularly likely to persist as offenders, and that they commit increasingly serious crimes as they grow older [Farrington 1996; Utting 1996]. By intervening preventively at the primary stage, CHANCE had the potential to nip their criminal career in the bud in a highly cost-effective way.

The primary school stage also offered a number of other potential long-term advantages. First, because almost all children in the UK attend primary school, teachers are in a position to help CHANCE to identify suitable children in a more or less uniform way and to provide a partner for CHANCE mentors' work with the children. Secondly, children of this age are relatively receptive to adult influence - arguably more so than they will be when they reach secondary school age. Thirdly, they are sufficiently cognitively mature to be able to understand social rules and to participate actively in social communication and learning.

## Training community volunteers to become mentors who deliver the intervention programme to the children.

The word 'mentor' comes from Homer's Odyssey. Ulysses appointed Mentor to be tutor-adviser to his son and guardian of his estates while he was fighting the Trojan war. More specifically, the approach chosen by CHANCE resembles contract mentoring, where a mature, experienced individual provides a supportive relationship, role model and trusted guide for a vulnerable younger person for a predefined period, with preset goals [Morton-Cooper & Palmer 1996].

The last few years have seen an explosion of interest in the idea and use of mentors, so that a UK National Mentoring Network, with a regular newsletter [Mentoring News, 2000], now exists. For the most part, the focus has been on the use of mentors to support professional training or development, such as teacher- or nurse-training. In the health field alone, a recent review by Oliver, Aggleton & Rivers [2000] identified over 1000 publications and reports on mentoring. Despite this number, the authors found virtually no controlled trials and only one systematic longitudinal evaluation of mentoring, which was of a qualitative nature. It seems fair to say that this represents the current picture. There is a great deal of enthusiasm, but as yet little systematic evidence, about the effectiveness, or limitations, of mentoring.

In relation to CHANCE, the issue is not professional development, but whether community volunteers can be trained to be effective in supporting and redirecting the development of a particularly challenging and disadvantaged group of young children. Here, too, there is a dearth of systematic evidence.

Arguably the best known English project involving mentors, the Dalston Youth Project, targets the secondary age-range and has so far received only a provisional evaluation of project implementation [Clarke & Tarling 1998]. How far it helps the youths who receive it is not yet known. The Edinburgh Volunteer Tutors Organisation, like CHANCE, uses adults to befriend and support young people, mostly in the eight to eleven year age-range, who are experiencing difficulties at home, at school or in the community. The recent evaluation of this scheme provides helpful descriptions of mentor activities and concludes that the mentors are valued by the children, but does not report whether the children show demonstrable improvements as a result [Buist 2000].

Internationally, the best known mentor scheme is the Big Brothers Big Sisters programme in the United States, which targets the ten to sixteen year age range. This long-running programme has been evaluated, including the use of a randomised control trial to assign target children to mentor or control groups [Tierney, Grossman & Resch 1995]. The mentored youths' reports indicated that they were 46 per cent less likely to initiate drug use, 27 per cent less likely to initiate alcohol use, a third less likely to hit someone and truanted from school half as often, as the control youths. These results are clearly encouraging. However, all the findings so far come from reports by the mentored youths. There is no independent evidence, as yet, of demonstrable changes in their behaviour or activities [Tierney et al 1995].

In sum, the limited evidence available supports the hope that mentors can help troubled children, but does not clearly show how far they are likely to be able to assist changes in primary school-aged children who are deliberately selected because of severe problems. It follows that CHANCE is innovative in exploring the use of mentors in this way.

## The mentor programme's policies.

The CHANCE child mentor programme was designed to have two plausible, clearly defined stages. In the first few weeks, the mentor's primary goal was to establish a trusting and supportive relationship with his, or her, target child. As well as compatibility with the concept of mentoring, this goal is supported by evidence that close relationships protect children, that is, reduce the likelihood that they will develop, and sustain, antisocial behaviour over the long term [Rutter & Garmezy 1983]. For CHANCE, this relationship was considered to be valuable in its own right and to provide the foundation for change.

Once a relationship was established, the mentor was expected to move on to an individualised, solution-focused intervention, which concentrated on identifying and changing the child's problem behaviour and re-directing development, rather than seeking to identify the original causes of the problem behaviour. The solution-focused approach drew on the theory of 'brief therapy' and ideas of Selekman [1997]. This approach has much in common with behavioural methods, which have proved to be particularly effective in resolving antisocial behaviour [Webster-Stratton & Hammond 1997]. By aiming to teach children life skills which encourage independence, active learning and a sense of personal mastery, CHANCE was designed to share some features with the High Scope intervention project, which proved outstandingly successful in the USA [Schweinhart & Weikart 1993].

## The programme's potential cost-effectiveness

A major advantage of using community volunteers as mentors is precisely that they are volunteers, allowing a programme which is potentially low in cost. In judging CHANCE's effectiveness, the critical question is not whether mentors are always successful, but whether they are sufficiently successful to justify the programme's cost – and whether they are more or less cost-effective than the alternatives.

The potential cost-effectiveness of CHANCE also has to be evaluated against the background of the human and financial costs of anti-social behaviour, exclusion and crime. While these costs are difficult to measure accurately, the Audit Commission has estimated that youth crime alone costs public services £1 billion a year, while the process of sentencing by itself costs £2500 per case [Audit Commission 1996]. These figures highlight the potential for cost effectiveness if the CHANCE intervention is successful.

# 3 The Implementation of the mentor programme

## Aims of this stage of the evaluation

In the long-term, CHANCE's effectiveness can be evaluated by measures of social exclusion, antisocial behaviour, and criminal offending. If it is to make improvements in these long-term outcomes, it will need to achieve a number of intervening objectives along the way:

- to establish effective working relationships within the CHANCE team, between the team and management committee, and between the project and Islington's schools, social service, police, education and health agencies;
- to recruit, vet, train, monitor and support the project's mentors;
- to identify and recruit the target children and their families, match them with mentors, and maintain their participation in the project;
- to develop record keeping systems which keep track of its activities;
- to keep within its planned budgets.

Accordingly, our goal during the first part of the evaluation was to establish whether the project was being implemented properly. Specifically, we had the following aims:

1. To establish whether CHANCE was being managed effectively, so that these initial objectives were being achieved in practice.
2. To assess whether the project met with the approval of its stakeholders, including those who originally conceived of it, the project team and management committee and the families and schools affected by it. Did the project hold true to the original vision and was it working from their point of view?
3. To describe and evaluate the mentors, children, and the mentoring process.
4. To lay the foundations for phase 2 of the evaluation, by assessing whether the mentors were building trusting relationships which could provide the basis for a more lasting change.

## Methodological approach

With formative evaluation purposes in mind, we participated in the CHANCE management committee meetings and provided guidance, as well as maintaining regular contact with the CHANCE team. We also assembled research evidence, together with lessons about good practice and examples of forms and documents from other mentor and crime prevention projects, so that CHANCE could build on these.

To evaluate the project's implementation at this stage in its development, we interviewed a range of its stakeholders, using semi-structured interviews, at the end of the evaluation's first year. In each case, we asked about (i) their visions for CHANCE; (ii) their views on whether it was working; (iii) whether any improvements were needed.

Those interviewed included: all three members of the CHANCE team; three members of the management committee (two of whom were senior policemen who had been involved from CHANCE's inception, the third a senior member of the Islington Education Welfare Department); six school teachers who had referred children to CHANCE; 16 mentors, 16 mentees (the mentored children), and 16 mentees' mothers, drawn at random from the group currently receiving mentoring. An attempt was made to interview fathers, but many children were cared for by single mothers, or fathers were unavailable. Each stakeholder interview had questions specific to that group, but other questions were duplicated so that we could compare the different views. Lastly, we examined the CHANCE records of the procedures involved in running the project. Details of the methods and findings are included in our first report [St James-Roberts & Samlal Singh 1998]. The main findings were as follows:

## Findings

### *Project management: strengths and concerns*

The CHANCE project team was considered professional, well-organised, and highly committed by all its stakeholders including, importantly, the teachers and head teachers who came into contact with it. The team had clearly defined roles, good working relationships, and worked effectively together. As well as professionalism, the schools valued CHANCE's rapid response. Instead of the weeks or months they were used to waiting when contacting social or educational psychology services, CHANCE provided a quick, reliable service. There was evidence that teachers would cooperate with the scheme and were keen to work in partnership with the CHANCE mentors.

The project team considered that they were supported by an effective management committee. Meetings occurred at appropriate intervals, were effectively run, and achieved the desired results. Members were available when needed and career development goals were being recognised.

Our own observations echoed this view. Because of the problems experienced by some other projects, it is worth identifying the features of the management committee which appeared to underlie its effectiveness. These included:

**Commitment:** members conveyed ownership, attended meetings, took on and completed tasks, supported each other and the project team.

**Seniority and expertise:** which allowed them to implement decisions and provided the necessary management skills.

**Representativeness and local knowledge:** by representing the various key agencies, including the police and education, they were able to draw on a wide range of local knowledge, backed up by a network of contacts and sources.

Other practical issues, such as insurance cover for the project and mentors, were also properly implemented and the project was keeping within its financial budgets.

As might be expected, there were changes in the membership both of the project team and management committee during the three years of the evaluation, while the project moved its premises within Islington for space and financial reasons. The changes included replacement of the chair of the management committee and the project co-ordinator (a post developed into chief executive), in both cases because career prospects led to emigration abroad.

For the most part, these and other challenges were used constructively, based on a clearly formulated long-term plan, indicating that CHANCE as a whole exhibited considerable resiliency. For example, the replacement chair of the management committee was recruited from business, to facilitate business planning.

Although our evaluation was largely positive, there were also areas where the day-to-day management of the project raised concerns.

1. The attempt to employ a part-time administrator was unsuccessful, so that a succession of individuals with limited qualifications stayed with the project for short periods. An effective administrator was needed to chase up and keep the records needed for management purposes, maintain the project's contacts with other groups (including the evaluators), and free up the CHANCE team from routine administrative chores. This is receiving renewed attention at the time of writing this report.

2. Although some written materials existed, much of the project was written up in outline form or was only in the heads of the project team. This and team's small size made the project vulnerable to the loss of staff. Written manuals which fully and explicitly documented how CHANCE worked were needed if the project was to be carried forward and disseminated. This recommendation was acted upon, so that a website which identifies the mentor training and other manuals used by CHANCE can be found at: http://www.chanceuk.com

3. Although CHANCE had established good working relationships with a number of local agencies, its links with health and, particularly, social services remained inadequate. Many of the target children had multiple problems, including health and social difficulties, while the inability to benefit from a concerted approach was an obvious weakness. Concerns about confidentiality prevented records from being shared, even though parents were willing to give consent to this. These problems were not specific to CHANCE, and were probably exacerbated by the re-organisation of local social and health services taking place at the time. They continue to be a source of concern and it seems likely that policy changes at government and local levels will be needed to remedy this.

4. During years two and three of its three-year funding, CHANCE began to focus on raising money for its continued existence and expansion. In addition, it piloted the planned child-peer and parent-support schemes. Each of these was successful, and funding for continuation and expansion was secured. However, in combination with the changes in location and personnel, these commitments over-stretched the CHANCE team, with the result that a shortfall occurred in the numbers receiving and completing mentoring. As the existing funding drew to a close, the project decided that it would be unethical to take on cases which it could not guarantee to complete, worsening the recruitment shortfall.

Although there are lessons for project management, it is important to point out that these difficulties were to a large extent the consequences of the three-year funding given to CHANCE. It is probably not possible to establish a project of this complexity within three years, while long-term funding arrangements and transitions need to be built in from the outset, so that pursuing funding does not interfere with the project's work. We will return to the issue of funding in Section 5.

## The stakeholders' vision for the mentor programme

Because of the ambiguity surrounding the notion of mentors and the diverse backgrounds of the project's stakeholders, we anticipated that there would be limited agreement about the project's aims and the role of mentors in bringing these about. In practice, we found that, broadly speaking, the stakeholders' expectations for the mentors shared a good deal of common ground. The most commonly used descriptors were:

**To provide vulnerable children with a trusting relationship and guide;** a support; a positive role model; someone for this child; someone to talk to, to turn to when needed; who helps the child to explore his feelings. Friendship with a purpose. An advocate; mediator; trained listener. Someone with life experience. As one mentor put it, *"It's harder being ten than 42"*.

**To build up this child's confidence; increase self-esteem;** someone who gives respect; who is non-manipulative; no hidden agenda; who makes this child special.

**To provide someone who sets boundaries and helps the child to recognise them;** to help with this child's behaviour; control flareups; teach him to stop, look and think.

**To provide an early, transforming intervention;** assist with change; help the child to look at things in a different way. To introduce alternatives; open up choices; new ways of behaving and being. *"Someone to help my son get on in life."*

It is apparent that the stakeholders expected that there would be changes both in the children's psychological capabilities and behaviour as a result of mentoring.

As well as these shared visions, two additional ideas were raised by some stakeholders. The first - an idea common to three of the 16 mothers - was that CHANCE should fulfil an educational purpose. These mothers saw their sons' problems as educational in origins. This raises the question of the mentors' role boundaries, to which we will return below. For one member of the management committee, the need for CHANCE arose from the lack of coordination between the statutory services. Professionalism had led to compartmentalisation: pigeonholing which prevented communication and delivery of services; crisis management instead of prevention. An advantage of mentors mentioned by several stakeholders was that they were not part of the statutory services and so did not pose a threat. From a mother's point of view, they had not come to take her child away.

## Mentor recruitment, vetting, training, monitoring and support

CHANCE recruited volunteers about four times a year, mostly via advertisements in local newspapers and existing contacts. A typical intake of 20 potential mentors was then trained over four days on two successive weekends.

Because the CHANCE mentors were community volunteers who were assigned to work with primary school-aged children, careful selection and vetting of mentors was vital. The methods used in vetting met Home Office and other guidelines for good practice.

Around 60 per cent of potential mentors dropped out between first enquiry and the end of training. Although this seems a high proportion, it is in line with figures from other mentor schemes [Tierny et al 1995] and it is sensible that dropouts should occur before mentors are matched with mentees. The dropout figures can be considered evidence that CHANCE selected its mentors rigorously, which is desirable.

The mentors' training is described in more detail on the project website: (http://www.chanceuk.com). Talks, videos and role playing were used to teach practical ideas and strategies based on solution-focused models of intervention [Selekman 1997]. The mentors themselves rated the training highly and considered the contents and length appropriate to get them started. In the mentors' words, the CHANCE team were:

*"Very professional; approachable; organised; knowledgeable; knew what they were doing, what they were looking for; professional but relaxed."*

*"They provided convincing ideas, backed up with practical examples and strategies."*

*"The training they gave was tough - they had high expectations."*

*"They were enabling, but quite clear what they expected and what they wanted from me."*

Once training is finished, a potential pitfall for mentor projects is leaving mentors to their own devices. To avoid this, the project team has to accept the responsibility for setting up an explicit framework for regular contacts and checks. To CHANCE's credit, this structure was in place. Initially, contacts were weekly, reducing to monthly once mentors were established. Mentor and CHANCE kept records of plans for the mentor/mentee meetings, what actually took place, and targets for future meetings. Progress was monitored and updated and the records provided the agenda for supervision sessions between a CHANCE project worker and mentor. If a mentor did not check in with CHANCE after the agreed interval, CHANCE followed this up. Both mentors and the CHANCE team were satisfied with these arrangements.

## The mentors' characteristics

Over 80 per cent of the mentors recruited by the project were women, the majority being Caucasian and 25 to 40 years of age. Like other similar programmes [Ivers 1999], CHANCE experienced difficulty in attracting volunteers who were male or non-Caucasian. The main reasons given for volunteering were the desire to help children, personal and career development, and the wish to 'give something back'. Several mentors mentioned key occasions when they had received support, which they wished to repay.

Although we have not found any empirical support for this view, it is widely believed that a mentor's gender and cultural background will critically affect whether a mentee identifies with the mentor and, consequently, the success of the relationship. Mentor schemes vary in how they match mentor with mentee, with some allowing mentees to exert a degree of choice. CHANCE assigned mentors, taking ethnic, religious and other factors into account so far as their stock of mentors allowed.

In practice, this 'matchmaker' approach seemed to work well in most cases. Most mentors, mentees and mentees' mothers we interviewed did not consider gender, ethnicity or religion to be critical considerations: the mentor's personal characteristics and commitment were more important. Most, too, were satisfied with their assigned mentor.

Although this finding applied in most cases, around 20 per cent of mothers reported that the mentor's gender or religious or cultural background was crucial in their case. CHANCE was able to take account of this in some, but not all cases. It is likely that this contributed to some of the cases where mentoring broke down. It does not seem to have been a common reason for mentoring failure, perhaps because the young age of CHANCE mentees made a 'maternal' mentor suitable, while most mentees were Caucasian. However, it was a source of concern for a minority of families.

## The mentees' characteristics

Most CHANCE-mentored children were recruited by teacher-referral from primary schools in Islington wards which met government criteria for social and economic deprivation. An initial concern was that, although the children fulfilled deprivation and need criteria, many did not exhibit behavioural or other signs which put them at increased risk of later criminal behaviour. A literature search showed that externalising behaviour problems, including conduct disorder, hyperactive behaviour, and problems with social and peer-relationships, were widely considered to be the best single predictors of persistent problems and crime [Bennett, Lipman, Racine & Offord 1998].

As a result, CHANCE adopted Goodman's (1997) Strengths and Difficulties Questionnaire (SDQ), a revision of Rutter's widely used Children's Behaviour Questionnaire, in July 1997. Particularly when completed by teachers, the SDQ provides a total behaviour problem score and subscores for conduct problems, relationship problems and hyperactivity which enable children with problem behaviour to be identified reliably. Using the normative scores available for the SDQ, CHANCE selected children who exceeded the UK 80th centile for problem behaviour to receive mentors.

Although the SDQ scores were the primary selection criteria, all the children came from socially and economically deprived areas, while family, demographic, educational, social and other risk indices were also collected for each child and included in selection. Table 1, based on CHANCE records of the children receiving mentoring in 1997/1998, summarises the results. These confirm that most children selected using the SDQ had multiple risk factors, adding further to the likelihood of criminal behaviour in the long-term [Graham & Bowling 1995].

***TABLE 1 Description of the CHANCE mentored children***

(all the children came from schools in areas of Islington which met government social and economic deprivation indices)

| TEACHER-REPORTED BEHAVIOUR | | OTHER CHARACTERISTICS | |
|---|---|---|---|
| Above UK 80th centile for behaviour problems: | 100% | Age at referral: | 6-10 years |
| hyperactive: | 91% | School exclusion: | 50% |
| Conduct problems: | 82% | Boy: | 97% |
| Social problems: | 62% | Free school meals: | 82% |
| Peer problems: | 59% | Single mothers: | 50% |
| Emotional problems: | 44% | Ethnicity: | |
| | | White: | 50% |
| | | Black: | 21% |
| | | Asian: | 10% |
| | | Mixed/other: | 19% |

## The process of mentoring: what do mentors do?

A typical mentor-mentee meeting lasted for two to four hours once a week, usually a weekend morning or afternoon, giving an average of about 120 hours over a year. Most mentors and mentees and their mothers were comfortable with the frequency and duration of the meetings, recognising the practical constraints. The most common activities reported were walks, sports and activities in the park; visits to the cinema, theatre or zoo; home activities such as cooking (in some cases at the mentor's home), puzzles, making things, computer games; visits to libraries or museums; homework; and just talking. A few mentors involved their mentees in activities with their own children. As well as their mentee, most mentors had regular contact with the mentees' mothers. Contact with other family members was intermittent. Some minor jealousy among siblings without mentors was reported, but no serious clashes with other family or household members were found.

## Building trusting relationships

The intended first goal for mentors was to establish a trusting relationship with their mentee. Although partly a measure of the programme's outcomes, the building of trusting relationships was examined at this stage, since CHANCE intended the relationships to provide a platform for changes in the children.

Because of the children's ages, we used open-ended questions to ask whether and why they liked their mentor and whether they felt the mentor liked them, followed by a set of standard questions with a menu of answers. Some children showed evidence of a halo effect, answering all questions positively. Others showed more discrimination, for instance by saying that a mentor helped them to control their temper, but not with school work. Just one child consistently reported unfavourably: "I don't like anything about her".

Almost all the remaining children answered "a lot" when asked whether their mentor:
(i) listens to me; (ii) is fair; (iii) is friendly; (iv) is honest – someone I can trust.
Almost all felt that their mentor liked them a lot.
Their spontaneous answers included statements such as:

*"She's kind* (this was mentioned often). *Lovable. Takes me out. Helps me a lot. Fun to do things with. Good for me. She gave me a pen.*

*She makes me feel good; she asks me what I want to do.*

*Every way she's a good friend to me; she's very, very good.*

*I talk to* (mentor) *a lot; she talks to me, answers questions.*

*She makes things better; shows me the way to find the answer. I've learned to control my feelings; not to get into a tantrum. She teaches me to count to ten.*

*She helps me to get on with work and finish it; not to be rude to teacher. Not to shout out; to put up my hand. I can talk to teacher now. She talks to my teacher.*

*She explains the consequences. I've learned to deal with disappointments."*

These findings provide evidence that the CHANCE mentor programme was successful in achieving its first goal, of building affectionate and trusting relationships between the children and their mentors.

One possible negative consequence of the children's involvement in CHANCE could be stigmatisation: that is, teasing or victimising by children, relations or family friends because of the mentor's presence. Except for one grandmother who did not approve, none of the mothers or children reported evidence of stigmatisation. If anything, the existence of a mentor conferred status, perhaps because of the associated attention and outings.

## Implementing the solution-focused stage of mentoring

It is easy to understand how activities such as walking in the park or swimming could foster bonds between mentor and mentee, but less clear how they could redirect development or provide a solution to the child's problems. To evaluate this, we asked the mentors about their immediate and longer-term goals for the meetings, and how the meetings were designed to meet the goals. To probe more closely, we followed an open-ended question with a list of possible goals. Mentors and other stakeholders were asked to prioritise these goals and to make explicit how they should be achieved. This exercise was chiefly intended to elicit the stakeholders' concepts. At a concrete, operational, level, did they have thought-through ideas on how to identify and prioritise solutions and about what mentors should actually do to achieve them?

Perhaps not surprisingly, the stakeholders varied widely in how many goals they identified and in which ones they prioritised. More worryingly, the mentors varied almost as much in the clarity of their formulations. Some planned their meetings with mentees with specific goals and a clearly worked out strategy in mind. Others appeared to turn up for meetings without a great deal of forethought and little overall idea of where the meetings were going or the steps needed to get there. Some mentors saw themselves as the link between home and school, attended school regularly, took part in case-conferences, and had set up a close working liaison with their mentee's teachers. Others were uncertain how to help with schoolwork, and how much to support the child, or to support the mother in order to help the child. Five mothers reported needing more help for themselves. In contrast, others spoke warmly of their own close relationship with the mentor: "an angel"; "I could tell her anything". In one outstanding case, the mother spoke highly of the regular feedback on her child's problems and progress the mentor provided. The mentor went out of her way to schedule meetings with the mother, thereby increasing her sense of involvement.

To some extent, it is to be expected that mentors will vary in their activities because of their mentee's individual circumstances and their own constraints. However, it is not easy to explain some mentors' lack of clearly defined goals in this way. Moreover, four of the 16 mentors interviewed expressed concerns about their role boundaries, with the chief concern being the mentees' educational needs. They wanted more detailed child assessments, together with access to specialist resources or training which would meet the needs of specific cases.

A case-example may help to illustrate the sort of difficulties which mentors faced:

*The mentee in this case was an emotionally withdrawn eleven year-old boy with English language and learning, as well as antisocial behavioural, problems. His mother believed that his difficulties stemmed mainly from his academic problems at school and, in effect, was looking for an academic tutor for her son. She also felt that the assigned mentor was too inexperienced and 'soft' in her approach to her son: she was looking for a firm structure and discipline. The mentor was unprepared for a child who was so hard to get through to and felt a need for counselling skills and training in how to tutor English and maths, none of which were available. She also considered that the mother's unreliability was a part of the problem. The task of supporting and tutoring the mentee, liaising between school and family, and coping with the uncooperative mother, was daunting for the mentor.*

In other cases, mentors had to contend with a mother's chronic mental health problems, and children on the Protection Register because of family violence. They wanted guidance on how far to focus on mother, family or child.

The question these findings raise is about mentors' role boundaries. It is possible that mentors' roles should be solely to provide a supportive relationship for their mentees, and this could be considered to be consistent with their volunteer status. However, this does not seem compatible with the idea of solution- focused mentoring. Children who have behaviour problems do commonly have multiple difficulties, including family and special educational needs [Robins & Rutter 1990], while poor parenting and educational achievement are risk factors for a criminal outcome [Utting 1996]. In principle these are worthy targets for a solution-focused intervention, but it is less clear whether they are realistic goals for mentors, particularly where these are community volunteers. CHANCE could consider using stricter selection criteria in order to weed out the most difficult cases. However, to do so might, in the end, defeat its objects. The point is that such multiple problems are characteristic of this group of children.

In sum, the interviews with mentors identified some uncertainty in what to target and how to deliver the solution-focused stage of mentoring. An examination of the mentors' and projects' records reinforced this impression of heterogeneity. Although outstanding examples of good practice existed, the mentors varied considerably. To some extent, these limitations may be inherent in the use of volunteers. However, they appeared also to reflect a lack of explicit, workable, guidelines about the solution-focused stage of mentoring on CHANCE's part. The mentors' goals were defined in broad rather than concrete, terms, so that it was unclear what criteria a mentor would use to gauge needs, progress or arrival at a goal.

## Bringing mentoring to a close

A feature of contract mentoring is that the duration of the mentor-mentee relationship is agreed from the outset. Given the age and nature of CHANCE mentees, questions arose about the most appropriate duration and when and how the issue of ending the relationship was to be raised and resolved. At least potentially, unplanned withdrawal of a mentor's support for a young and vulnerable child could be highly damaging.

CHANCE's policy was that mentoring should aim to last for about a year, with extensions in special circumstances. This was a compromise between the need to attract mentors, the need to provide the children with sufficient support while avoiding dependency, and the costs of the programme, which would be increased by a longer period. The idea that support should be provided for a predefined period was also consistent with the idea of brief therapy, which underlay much of CHANCE's thinking [Selekman 1997]. The objective was to help the mentee to achieve self-reliance, which would promote independent development.

To highlight this expectation, a mentee graduation was implemented in 1998. Early in the relationship, mentors introduced the idea that mentoring would only last as long as a child needed it, so that its completion should be seen as evidence of a positive achievement – that the child had 'moved on'. A graduation ceremony was included, where both children and parents were invited together with CHANCE staff and outside visitors, with each child being given a certificate of achievement, together with a simple camera to record the event. These occasions proved highly enjoyable all round.

Although it is reasonable to have a target length of time in mind for mentoring, it is arguable whether a year is appropriate or whether time should be the deciding consideration. Since mentoring was intended to end when its goals had been reached, the issue again raised was what constituted a solution to a child's problems, and what evidence a mentor should use in deciding that this solution had been achieved.

## Summary of the implementation findings.

In sum, our evaluation of the implementation of the CHANCE mentor programme identified many strengths. The schools and other stakeholders in the programme considered that it met their expectations and was highly professional and thorough. Many aspects of the management and delivery of the programme were of an outstandingly high standard. There was evidence that the first goal of mentoring, achievement of a trusting relationship between mentor and child, was being achieved.

Our chief concern at this stage was about the implementation of the second, solution-focused, element of mentoring. Delivery appeared to be patchy and CHANCE policies and guidelines for this phase of mentoring needed clarification and development. In keeping with the purposes of evaluation, the findings were fed back to CHANCE to assist them in continuing to develop evidence-based policies and practices.

# 4 The programme's effectiveness in achieving changes in the children

## Aims and methodological approach of this part of the evaluation

To achieve its target outcomes, CHANCE needed to deliver its mentor programme successfully to around 40 children per year. Whether the project achieved this target could be considered a question of implementation, but is considered below since it also bears directly on CHANCE's effectiveness, and cost-effectiveness, in achieving its targeted outcomes.

The aim of measuring changes in children raises conceptual and methodological challenges. Issues arise about who should be asked, and the most appropriate forms of data, methods, and research designs.

Many evaluations of community intervention programmes collect their data from stakeholders, such as the children and families participating in the programme, after the programme is over. Although their views of the value and effects of the programme are of central importance, it is arguable whether they provide a sufficiently stringent evaluation. For a variety of reasons, individuals who take part in intervention programmes may be inclined to view them positively, and this view may influence their recollection and report of the programme's effects. This implies a need to obtain supplementary, independent, information.

In a review of 'What Works in Preventing Criminality', Graham [1998] argues "It is also recognised that, to be effective, programmes should target behavioural change and not just changes in attitudes, values or knowledge." (P.16). His point is well taken. The psychological literature abounds with examples of studies which have changed people's psychological reports without changing their behaviour. While perceived psychological change may give rise to behavioural change, it does not necessarily do so.

The importance of behavioural measures for the evaluation also derived from the use of behaviour problem scores to select the mentored children. Since existing behaviour problems are among the best predictors of long-term problems, reductions in this area would provide firm evidence that the mentor programme was on track towards achieving its long-term goals.

To take account of these issues so far as possible within the resources available, three main forms of information were collected:

1. To obtain the children's and parents' evaluations of the children's progress, we interviewed them individually after mentoring was completed about the programme's effects on the children. Semi-structured interviews were used, with questions and verbatim answers being followed by answers chosen from a menu of standard ratings. As well as the benefits of mentoring, parents were asked questions based on the SDQ items, to assess how much their child had changed in each of the 5 main behavioural areas assessed by the SDQ (conduct problems, hyperactivity, peer problems, emotional problems, prosocial behaviour)

2. In view of the concerns about the solution-focused stage of mentoring raised earlier, we examined the children's graduation certificates, which recorded the children's achievements from the mentors' and project's point of view.

3. To provide standardised, independent measures of the generalisability of the changes, we obtained measures from their teachers of the children's behaviour, school attendance and academic performance at baseline (before mentoring started) and after their graduation from the mentor programme. These were supplemented by open-ended questions, which allowed the teachers to record areas of individual progress.

As explained below, these measures were obtained for 25 of the 32 children who successfully completed mentoring. In view of their behaviour problems, it was expected that the mentored children would receive a variety of additional interventions at school, and possibly outside, during the mentoring period. To allow the results of the mentor programme to be distinguished, a matched 'comparison' group of children with comparable problems who were not given mentors were assessed on the same measures of behaviour, attendance and academic performance at school, before and after the equivalent period. These children were selected from schools in areas of Islington which met the same social and economic deprivation criteria as the CHANCE feeder schools. The criteria used in selecting and matching them with the mentored children are given in Table 2. As the figures show, the mentored and comparison children were closely matched at baseline on age, SDQ scores, gender and ethnicity.

***Table 2. Selection criteria used to match the mentored and comparison (non-mentored) groups of children.***

(All the children came from schools in areas of Islington which met government social and economic deprivation criteria).

| | Mentored Children (N=25) | Comparison (non-mentored) Children (N=25) |
|---|---|---|
| Mean(sd) Age | 101 (19) months | 97 (14) months |
| Ethnicity | 44% White<br>56% Non-White | 40% White<br>60% Non-White |
| Gender | 84% (21) boys | 72% (18) boys |
| Mean (sd) Total SDQ Score* | 25 (3.3) | 23 (4.0) |

* U.K. 80th centile score = 15.

## Findings

### Numbers enrolled in the CHANCE mentor programme

To achieve its target outcomes, the mentor programme needed to graduate around 40 children per year. Table 3 summarises the throughput of children referred to the mentor programme during the 30-month period from August 1997 to March 2000. Instead of the 80-100 children who should have completed mentoring successfully during this period, only 32 did so.

***Table 3. Throughput figures for the children referred to CHANCE between August 1997 and March 2000.***

| NUMBER OF CHILDREN: | |
|---|---|
| Referred | 122 |
| Who declined to take part | 2 |
| Not accepted by CHANCE | 49 |
| Accepted by CHANCE | 71 |
| Completed mentoring successfully* | 32 |
| Mentoring terminated prematurely for external reasons | 5 |
| Mentoring terminated prematurely because it broke down | 9 |
| Mentoring currently continuing | 12 |
| Awaiting a mentor | 13 |

*In 7 of the 32 cases, a second mentor was needed in order to complete the mentoring

A substantial proportion (44%) of the 122 referred children were not accepted by CHANCE, but most were excluded because they did not meet the SDQ selection criteria, providing evidence that the project screened its referrals effectively. Also in keeping with CHANCE policy, a few others were excluded because of a history of violence or other family features which might place mentors at risk. Because CHANCE recruited only 71 children during this 30-month period, a recruitment shortfall was one factor which limited the number of successfully mentored children. This was probably due to the other commitments CHANCE took on during the second and third years of its initial funding since, at the time of writing, the numbers are increasing.

Although the low rate of recruitment certainly contributed to the graduation shortfall, Table 3 suggests that neither the total number of referrals, nor the number accepted into the mentor programme, were the overriding limiting factors. Since the average length of mentoring for the successfully mentored children was 11.5 months, prolonged mentoring did not seem to be the reason either. In five cases, the failure to complete mentoring successfully was due to factors beyond the project's control, such as a move of the family outside the geographic area, but this, too, was comparatively rare.

As Table 3 illustrates, another consideration was the relatively high proportion of cases where the first mentor relationship was unsuccessful, requiring the child's re-assignment to a new mentor, or where mentoring broke down completely because the mentor or child (and child's parents) withdrew. Nine of 71 mentoring relationships (13%) broke down completely, while a further seven required reassignment of a child to a second mentor, giving 16 of 71 cases – over 20 per cent – where the first mentor-mentee relationship did not thrive. This was time-consuming, costly and unsatisfactory from everybody's point of view. On the evidence available, terminations appear to have been initiated about equally often by child/family and by mentors or project. In a few cases, termination had a clear basis, such as change in a mentor's career or, in one case, withdrawal of the mentor by the project because of concerns about her safety. In most cases, termination appeared to be due a breakdown of communication on one or both sides.

These figures testify to the difficulties involved in completing mentoring successfully with this challenging group of children. From a practical point of view, the main question they raise is how to increase the rate of successful completions. We will return to this, and to the associated issue of the cost of the mentoring programme, in Section 5.

**Mentees' and parents' evaluation of the mentees' progress**

Seven of the 32 children who graduated through mentoring completed their mentoring period before we began this stage of the evaluation, so that we were unable to collect immediate outcome data. We plan to include them in a longer-term follow up.

We approached all 25 remaining parents and children where children graduated successfully, and 24 sets of interviews were completed, 16 with mothers only, two with fathers only, two with both parents, two with grandparents, one with a mother and older sibling, and one with a foster-mother. The mentee was also interviewed separately in each case. Twenty one mentees were boys. Eighty per cent of their mentors were female, most within the 25-40 year age range. Two thirds of the mentors were white, a third from minority ethnic groups.

As in the implementation interviews, the parents were overwhelmingly positive about the professionalism of CHANCE, the mentors, and their child's experiences. Most parents felt that the mentor had turned out to be what they were looking for, but three were disappointed because of the mentor's gender or ethnic background. All but one felt that the mentor had had a good influence on their child.

Table 4 summarises the parents' answers to the more specific questions about the effects of mentoring on their children's behaviour. The responses were mixed and there were no areas where most parents considered the children to be much improved. In most areas, about half the children were considered to have improved and half stayed the same. The most noteworthy improvements were in being considerate towards others' feelings, in developing confidence, and in making friends. In the parents' own words:

*"He is more confident than he used to be."*

*"He has a lot more patience."*

*"He is calmer than he used to be."*

*"He had problems making friends – now he understands people's feelings more. He is more communicative and shows more respect for people. He is more positive about school."*

**Table 4. Parents' reports of changes in their children's behaviour (N=24).**

| | Much Improved | Bit Improved | Same | Worse* |
|---|---|---|---|---|
| Considerate of others' feelings | 9 | 4 | 9 | 1 |
| Helpful if someone hurt or upset | 6 | 4 | 12 | 1 |
| Thinks before acting | 2 | 8 | 11 | 2 |
| Distractible | 2 | 9 | 9 | 3 |
| Restless/ overactive | 5 | 6 | 11 | 1 |
| Fidgety/ squirmy | 0 | 7 | 15 | 1 |
| Tempers | 3 | 7 | 9 | 4 |
| Fights/ bullies other children | 4 | 5 | 12 | 2 |
| Lies/ cheats | 3 | 5 | 6 | 3 |
| Has at least 1 good friend | 7 | 4 | 12 | 0 |
| Nervous/ lacks confidence | 6 | 3 | 12 | 2 |

Parents could choose 'a bit worse' or 'much worse' but seldom chose the latter, so they are collapsed here. Where rows do not total 24, parents considered the question inapplicable.

Fourteen of the 24 parents considered that their child's attitude to school had improved and eleven identified an improvement in their own relationship with the school. Ten reported that their child was more willing to do homework and 12 improved progress at school. Eleven children had taken unauthorised days off school in the previous three months. Thirteen parents had been contacted by the school because of difficulties with their child in this three months. Four had received contacts from social services and three from the police for this reason.

The mentee children all reported that they liked their mentor 'a lot'. All reported that they trusted their mentor, that he/she was fair, friendly, and listened to what they said. All except one were sure that their mentor liked them. Three children had complaints:

*"At first, she didn't turn up because her job was too hard"*

*"He kept telling me what to do – sit down in the film"*

*"He took me to places I didn't like"*

Fewer children than parents said that their mentor had helped them to improve their school grades (eight 'a little' and only two 'very much'). Most (16) said that their mentor had helped them to learn to control their temper, to be more considerate (14), and to get on better with friends (14), parents (16) and teachers (16). Eighteen felt they had learned to say sorry when they had done something wrong, and 20 said they felt more confident and better about themselves.

## Achieving the solution-focus changes in the children

The graduation certificates of each of the successfully mentored cases were examined for evidence of the individual goals had been set and achieved. Each certificate listed the main areas in which progress had been made, according to the mentor and project's assessment of the child. The findings are summarised in Table 5

***Table 5. Achievements recognised on the mentees' graduation certificates.***

| Area of achievement | Number of certificates Listing this achievement |
|---|---|
| Getting on with others; Politeness, being considerate | 19 |
| Specific skills and competencies: e.g. sport, cooking, gardening | 15 |
| Control of emotions, tempers, moods | 10 |
| Broad cognitive competencies: Concentration, planning, persistence | 10 |
| School/educational skills: Reading, writing, spelling | 9 |
| Talking about own feelings | 6 |
| Life skills/learning to be responsible | 6 |
| Making friends | 5 |
| Developing confidence | 4 |

The most common goal was learning to get on with children and adults, which was listed as an achievement on the graduation certificates of most of the children. This included learning to be considerate, polite and to take turns and follow social rules. Improved emotional control, including control of tempers and moods, and ability to remain calm and cope with disappointments, was another common achievement. A number of children who had shown difficulty in communicating with others about their thoughts and feelings had made progress in this area.

The development of specific skills and competencies, presumably designed to raise self-confidence, was also recognised on most of the graduation records. The most common were sport skills, but individual children showed development in cooking and gardening. In a handful of cases, increases in confidence were explicitly singled out.

Another common area of achievement was in broad cognitive abilities, such as the ability to plan activities, and to concentrate and persist in achieving the desired outcomes. Progress in educational competencies, such as in reading, writing and spelling, was identified in 40 per cent of the children.

Improvements in life skills, including ability to use money, knowing the way around the neighbourhood, eating healthier foods, and going to bed on time, were noted in about a quarter of cases.

Lastly, the certificates identified individual strengths, such as a sense of humour, together with areas of progress in areas of vulnerability specific to the child. For example, one child had made progress in distinguishing strangers, where before he had been indiscriminately friendly.

These findings are largely consistent with the reports of the parents and mentees in suggesting that the mentors' main influence was to help the children to develop confidence, self-control and social awareness. In the absence of a control group, it is difficult to be sure how far these improvements reflect growing older, but the parents were certainly clear that the improvements were due to the child's mentor. A second question is whether the changes were substantial enough. In the absence of a benchmark which compares the children to some standards, it is hard to know whether these improvements in the children's competencies were sufficient to reduce the likelihood that they will have problems in the long term.

## Standardised assessments of attendance, behaviour and attainment at school

***Table 6. Measures obtained at baseline and outcome ages for both the mentored and comparison groups of children***

Strengths and Difficulties Questionnaires completed by teachers
Number of days absent, and excluded from school, in last 6 months.
Reading age.
Teacher National Curriculum level rating in English, science and maths.
Special Educational Needs/ Statementing status.
Teacher report of individual progress and problems in the last 6 months.

Table 6 summarises the measures collected at baseline and outcome ages for the successfully mentored and comparison groups of children. Strengths and Difficulties Questionnaire (SDQ) scores were used to measure changes in behaviour, while most of the remaining measures concern standardised assessments of attendance, academic performance, and special educational needs. Although CHANCE policies did not focus directly on academic abilities, these were targeted by some mentors and were identified as areas of progress by some parents and mentee graduation certificates. Academic measures were also included as indices of competencies known to reduce the risk of long-term antisocial behaviour, school exclusion and crime [Farringdon 1996, Utting 1996].

Lastly, to ensure that individual changes in the children not reflected in the standardised measures were recognised, teachers were asked in an open-ended question to record any other improvements, or problems, which each child had shown over the last six months.

Table 7 summarises the SDQ, behavioural, findings. The findings are clear-cut. Both the mentored and comparison children improved significantly in their behaviour scores over the period of approximately a year between baseline and outcome measures. However, the mean scores at outcome were still above the UK cut-off for behaviour problems, and the children who had mentors did not improve in behaviour any more, or less, than children who did not have mentors. As Table 7 shows, this was true both for their overall problem scores and for the individual area sub-scores. To ensure that individual cases were not misrepresented by the means, the data were also examined to identify the number of children whose scores had improved, worsened, or stayed the same. These figures, too, were similar in the two groups.

***Table 7. Strengths and Difficulties Questionnaire scores at baseline and outcome ages for the mentored and comparison groups of children.***

| | MENTORED GROUP | | COMPARISON GROUP | |
|---|---|---|---|---|
| | Baseline | Outcome | Baseline | Outcome |
| Mean (sd)<br>total difficulty score* | 24.5 (3.3) | 19.2 (7.2) | 23.4 (4.0) | 17.0 (8.1) |
| Mean (sd)<br>conduct sub-score | 5.6 (1.9) | 4.7 (2.7) | 5.8 (2.8) | 4.1 (3.1) |
| Mean (sd)<br>hyperactivity sub-score | 9.0 (1.3) | 7.7 (2.6) | 8.8 (1.6) | 6.8 (3.1) |
| Mean (sd)<br>Emotional sub-score | 4.6 (2.9) | 3.1 (3.0) | 4.0 (2.8) | 3.0 (2.5) |
| Mean (sd)<br>peer sub-score | 5.2 (2.0) | 3.6 (2.3) | 4.9 (2.2) | 3.0 (2.0) |
| Mean (sd)<br>Pro-social sub-score | 4.0 (2.4) | 4.7 (2.9) | 3.9 (3.0) | 5.5 (2.6) |

*Change between Baseline and Outcome scores is significant (repeated measures anova, $F = 25.772$, $df = 1$, $p<.001$), while group difference and group by change interaction are non-significant ($F=.202$, $p=.655$, and $F=1.62$, $p=.206$, respectively)

Table 8 summarises the children's school exclusion, attendance and reading score records at baseline and outcome ages. There are no significant differences between the mentored and comparison children on any of these measures. Other records, including teacher assessments of attainments in English, maths and science were also examined and failed to show group differences.

**Table 8. School exclusion, attendance and academic measures at baseline and outcome ages for the mentored and comparison groups of children.**

| | MENTORED GROUP (N=25) | | COMPARISON GROUP (N=25) | |
|---|---|---|---|---|
| | Baseline | Outcome | Baseline | Outcome |
| Number of children excluded from school in the last term | 3 | 2 | 5 | 3 |
| Mean number of sessions* absent from school | 11 | 27 | 11 | 23 |
| Mean (sd) reading age (months) | 92 (13) | 102 (18) | 87 (13) | 103 (17) |
| Number of children entered on Special Educational Needs Register | 16 | 18 | 19 | 21 |

* A session is a morning or afternoon.

At the outcome ages, almost all the children in both groups were receiving special support for their behavioural or educational difficulties, ranging from weekly reading support in school through full-time placement in a pupil referral unit. There was no obvious relationship between such help and the behavioural or academic measures, but the data are unsuitable for detecting this. Most children in both groups were on the Special Educational Needs Register.

Lastly, the teachers' individualised reports were scrutinised to identify areas of progress, or difficulty, not apparent in the standardised measures. Individual areas of progress were identified for four mentored and five comparison children, but there was no evidence that the mentored children showed superior gains.

## The CHANCE child-peer and parent-mentor schemes.

In keeping with its original proposal, CHANCE piloted both parent-mentor and child-peer schemes as supplements to its child-mentor programme during years two and three of its funding. The goal was that the mentored children would take part in social-skill building sessions with peers, while their parents would be offered the support of a parent-mentor. Both schemes were evaluated and found to be successful, but neither was implemented as a routine part of the CHANCE project. In the case of the peer-programme, improvements in social behaviour were observed, but transporting the children proved to be a stumbling block.

Because the number of CHANCE children in any one school at one time was small, transport was needed to bus children to a common location. The costs in staff time, vehicle hire, and insurance proved prohibitive.

The parent-mentor scheme involved eight 90-minute sessions delivered to parents of children who had child mentors over a period of about two months. It aimed to reduce perceived parenting stress, improve parents' engagement with their children, and teach skills for dealing with conflicts. It was taken up by about 60 per cent of the parents offered it. They reported improved confidence and ability to cope with their children, together with improvements in family interactions. The findings were promising, but the demands of running this scheme alongside the child mentor programme and the project's other commitments proved excessive. It was shelved for the time being, with the intention to re-introduce it at a later date. Reports of the evaluations of these two schemes are available from the authors.

## Costs of the CHANCE project.

In estimating the costs of Project CHANCE, the child-peer and parent-mentor schemes need to be taken into account. They were run by the project team with volunteer staffing, so that they represent potential additional outcomes or products of the programme, which could probably be achieved with only modest increases in cost. Since they have not proved viable up to the present, we will not include them in the estimates below. The costs below are largely, but not solely, the costs of running the child-mentor programme.

By dividing the total annual cost of running CHANCE by the number of children who receive mentors, it is possible to derive a figure for the approximate cost of providing a mentor. Based on 40 children completing mentoring successfully per year, this was targeted to be £3,000 per child in the Project's 1997-8 Annual Report, and was projected to eventually cost £2,500 per child. Since the project has not consistently achieved its target numbers, the cost was closer to £10,000 per child during the 30 month evaluation period but is currently falling as the numbers return towards the target levels.

In principle, figures of this kind can be used to compare different interventions for their cost-effectiveness. In practice, it is difficult to do so until a standard formula for this purpose is developed. Utting [1996] for example, lists costs for crime prevention programmes varying from a few hundred pounds to over 15 thousand pounds per child per year, but few projects provide accounts in enough detail to see what they include. In America, the Big Brothers Big Sisters Scheme is reported to cost $1000 for each youth who receives a mentor [Tierney et al 1995]. However, it is not clear what this estimate includes; for instance, whether it includes the cost of the project's salaries or premises, or how the American figures would translate into London terms.

In CHANCE's case, the cost of renting a premises in inner London accounted for 10 per cent of its total budget, staff costs around 80 per cent, and mentor-associated costs just 5 per cent of the budget each year. The bulk of CHANCE's cost was due to project staff salaries, but it is unlikely that the project could be delivered effectively by fewer or more junior staff.

As well as the cost per child, cost-effectiveness and cost-benefit analyses require that the effects of an intervention be known. A relatively costly intervention can be more cost-effective if it has results which are more substantial or long-lasting. To the best of our knowledge, none of the evaluations of mentor or crime prevention programmes published so far have used assessments as extensive as those included in the present report. The lessons from the American High Scope project are also relevant. The initial returns on this project were limited, but its long-term benefits have been among the most impressive achieved so far, with every $1 cost of the programme reported to result in a $7 saving in costs to the community [Schweinhart & Weikert 1993]. It is noteworthy that High Scope's effectiveness was under-valued in its initial evaluations – it took some time for the benefits to become clear.

For these reasons, it is not yet practicable to evaluate Project CHANCE's relative cost or value. What is clear is that CHANCE did not meet its own targets over this 30-month evaluation period, so that the attention currently being given to improving its numbers is timely. It is also apparent that the figures given above stand in marked contrast to the cost of crime to the community, so that the potential for saving in financial and human costs is considerable.

## Summary of the cost and effectiveness findings

During the 30 month period evaluated, Project CHANCE piloted parent-support and child-peer schemes and pursued funding for its continued existence, as well as running its core, child-mentor, programme. These goals were achieved and continued funding was obtained, but the added commitments over-extended the project. Fewer children than planned completed the mentor programme, with the result that it proved substantially more expensive than budgeted for. This is currently receiving attention.

Children who completed the programme were reported by their mentors, their parents, and by the children themselves, to show gains. The most consistent improvements were in the development of confidence, self-control and social awareness and relationships. These were promising developments, since they represent competencies which should help the children to control their behaviour and help them to get on with other children and adults, increasing their resiliency and reducing the risk of long-term problems.

To assess the generalisability of these improvements, we obtained independent measures of their school behaviour, attendance, exclusion, and academic performance before and after mentoring from school records and the children's teachers. The mentored children improved in their behaviour, but equivalent improvements were found in a group of matched comparison children who did not have mentors. Both groups continued to have serious problems.

# 5 Questions and lessons raised by the evaluation findings

By the completion of our evaluation, in March 2000, CHANCE had already implemented a remarkable and innovative mentor programme and achieved many of its goals. The programme was effectively run and valued by the families and schools who invested in it. There was clear evidence that the mentors' first goal, of building trusting relationships with their mentored children, was being achieved. The children, mentors and parents all reported some gains, particularly in the children's confidence, self-control, and social awareness and relationships.

There were three areas where the evaluation findings were more disappointing. First, the programme had not been delivered to the target numbers. Second, we were concerned about the implementation and effectiveness of the solution-focused stage of mentoring. Third, we did not find evidence that the improvements in the children identified at home had generalised to provide improvements in behaviour at school as a result of their mentoring. The aim below is to put the findings as a whole in context, and to bring out the lessons for similar projects and evaluations, in the future.

## Numbers graduating through the programme

CHANCE is not the only programme of its type to have had difficulty in achieving its planned numbers [Ivers 1999], but this shortfall adds substantially to the costs of mentor programmes, whereas a low cost is part of their appeal.

Because the numbers of mentors and children recruited set obvious limits on the number who can graduate, recruitment policies and practices are one area for project development. However, recruitment numbers are by no means the only constraint. An important finding was that 20% of the initial mentor-mentee relationships set up by CHANCE failed to thrive, while 13 per cent broke down completely. These rates seem at least as good as those of other mentor schemes [Grossman & Johnson 1998], while they undoubtedly reflect the particularly challenging nature of the children and families recruited into the programme. However, the question the figures highlight is how to improve the programme's completion and graduation rates. In turn, this draws attention to the processes involved in mentor selection, matching mentors with mentees, and monitoring and guiding their relationship.

In common with other mentor programmes, CHANCE has consistently had difficulty in recruiting sufficient male and non-Caucasian mentors. This appears to affect only a minority of cases, but is one potential area for improvement. Until recently, the main method of mentor recruitment has been newspaper advertisements, which have generated sufficient numbers, but failed to resolve the shortfall in male and minority group mentors. By changing the project's recruitment strategies, for instance by establishing links with businesses, universities and community groups, the shortfalls may be overcome and greater choice afforded. At the same time, there is a need for procedures which assess mentors and for record keeping and dissemination, so that projects can share their lessons about the mentor qualities, matching procedures, and supervisory arrangements, which lead to successful mentoring outcomes.

## The solution-focused stage of mentoring

CHANCE shares the aim of establishing a trusting and supportive adult-child relationship with other mentor programmes [Buist 2000; McGill 1999]. It is the second, solution-focused stage of its mentoring which is, arguably, its most distinct, innovative and potentially significant component. By utilising the mentor relationship as the foundation for solution-focused change, CHANCE coincides in its approach with behavioural interventions, which have been found to be effective in resolving behaviour problems in children and youth [Webster-Stratton & Hammond 1997]. Importantly, too, there is evidence that CHANCE is evolving a theoretical model of how this might work. That is, the goal for mentoring appears to be to promote the mentee's psychological competencies, particularly in emotion-regulation, planning and self-control, and in social awareness and relationships, in order to increase resiliency. These competencies are similar to those targeted by the American Fast Track programme, which has produced recent evidence of achieving them and improving behaviour as a result [Weissberg & Greenberg 1998].

In practice, our finding here was that the solution-focused stage of the CHANCE mentor programme was not successful in achieving the desired improvements in mentee behaviour, so far as this was judged by comparing their behaviour at school with the behaviour of other similar children. Both groups improved in behaviour over a year, but both continued to show serious behaviour problems at outcome, while the CHANCE mentored children did not improve more than their non-mentored peers.

It is important to point out that this is a stringent test. What is required is both psychological and behavioural change which is sufficiently generalised to have a demonstrable impact on behaviour at school. Very few intervention programmes of any kind have sought, or achieved, this so far. Nevertheless, in view of what is understood about the predictors of later antisocial behaviour and criminal activity, demonstrable improvement in behaviour across home and school settings is certainly a worthwhile goal.

It is possible that achieving behavioural change of this type and extent in such children is beyond the scope of mentoring, a point we will revisit below. Alternatively, as the findings have suggested, the problem may not be that the goal is unattainable, but rather that the solution-focused stage of mentoring was not being fully implemented at the time of this evaluation.

If mentors are to achieve changes in children's psychological competencies and resiliencies, the programme they are part of will need clear policies and guidelines for how this phase of mentoring is to be put into practical effect. The mentors will need concrete guidance on how to identify a target, such as emotion-regulation, and what steps to take towards promoting it. Just as important, the programme will need workable benchmarks to identify when a 'solution' has been achieved. Since children often improve in areas such as emotion regulation as they get older, the mentors need to be able to identify when an improvement is significant.

As an illustrative example, an attempt to measure the children's self-confidence was made early in this evaluation, using Harter & Pike's [1980] Pictorial Scales of Perceived Competence. This stemmed from the, widespread, belief that poor-self esteem is a problem for children with behaviour problems. In practice, the pilot findings indicated that the children had high self-esteem. Nor was this an isolated finding, since other studies, too, have found children with conduct disorder and hyperactivity to have high self-esteem [Edens et al 1999; Hoza et al 2000]. This may be because children with behaviour problems have a biased view of their own abilities, but it raises both the question of why mentoring with these children should aim to increase self-esteem, and of how any improvements might be measured. A clear theory is needed to specify which psychological competencies should be targeted by mentors, how they should achieve changes, and how the changes should be measured. The articulation of such theories of change, and of the associated assessment processes, is a task which requires a collaboration between evaluations and projects. Weissberg & Greenberg [1998] have summarised the approaches being trialed by other intervention initiatives, so that the challenge is to adapt them for mentor project and evaluation purposes.

## Dosage

The term 'dosage' refers to the amount of an intervention which is delivered [Henrich, Brown & Aber 1999]. The question here is whether some 40 meetings between mentor and mentee, totalling around 120 hours, is enough.

The period of around a year targeted by CHANCE represents a compromise between cost, the need to attract mentors, and hoped-for effectiveness, but is essentially arbitrary. Although there is some evidence that mentoring which lasts a year is more effective than shorter interventions [Grossman & Johnson 1998], it is not at all clear whether this is long enough for the type and age-group of children targeted here. Moreover, it is not unusual for mentoring to last for longer in other projects. McGill [1999] reports that the American Big Brothers Big Sisters scheme provides mentors for two-and-a-half years on average, while many mentor relationships last much longer.

Although a target length for mentoring is desirable, it is arguable whether it should be a year, or whether the length alone should be a primary criterion. As noted earlier, the critical consideration is that the targeted solution should be reached, while the length of time needed to do so is an empirical matter. Evidence is needed on the optimal mentoring dosage for different ages and types of children.

## Mentoring alone, or as part of an intervention package?

Until recently, CHANCE thinking about its mentor programme has been strongly influenced by 'Solution Therapy' approaches to intervention [Selekman 1997]. In essence, the principle is that a key intervention, lasting for a short while, should equip the recipient with competencies which promote resiliency.

The idea of a single, relatively brief intervention is attractive, particularly from a cost-effectiveness point of view. By developing mentoring independently, it should also be possible to learn more about its effectiveness, limitations, and costs, in supporting vulnerable children. This said, there are good reasons for doubting whether mentoring alone can provide sufficient support for such multiply disadvantaged children or, indeed, whether a single, child-focused, intervention is the best approach to adopt. As Graham [1998] puts it: '...it is now accepted that, to be effective, prevention programmes need to comprise a range of complementary measures which target multiple risk factors within the primary domains of a child's life' (P.16). The implication is that multiple interventions targeting both a child's psychological resources and environmental conditions are needed to achieve sustained progress. Rather than being delivered during a circumscribed period, they may need to be provided cumulatively to support development over prolonged periods of time.

Although it is important not to lose sight of the cost of intervention programmes, there is an argument that it would be best to demonstrate effectiveness first. If Graham's view is taken to heart – and it is shared by many others – the implication is that projects should try to use combined and cumulative interventions wherever possible.

In CHANCE's case, parent-mentor and child peer-group schemes have been piloted and found helpful in supporting parents and changing the children's social behaviour with peers, respectively. The effectiveness of combining these interventions, compared to mentoring alone, needs to be evaluated. Since most CHANCE children are referred by schools, while education may help to build competencies, a closer partnership between CHANCE mentors and teachers may also be worth pursuing.

## Evaluation design and methods

Although there has been much debate about the optimum design for evaluation purposes, there are signs of growing consensus. As Henrich et al [1999] point out, no single design is sufficient, so that research designs need to be combined to evaluate interventions adequately. Randomised Controlled Trials (RCTs), often regarded as the gold standard for trials of medical interventions, ask potential participants to give informed consent, assigning them afterwards at random to treatment or control groups. Given suitably large samples, this design maximises internal validity, because change solely in the experimental group can be clearly attributed to the intervention. The limitation is that the experimentally implemented programme is seldom the same as the programme as it is implemented in the everyday world. Moreover, it is not unusual for the majority of potential participants to refuse to take part in trials which require random assignment to the experimenters' chosen conditions [St James-Roberts et al 2001], with the consequence that the experimental results may not generalise to the target community.

Instead of a RCT, a quasi-experimental, matched group design was chosen here for evaluating the effects of CHANCE's mentor programme on children who successfully completed it. This design allows less certainty whether the mentoring intervention is responsible for any changes in the mentored group, relative to the matched children. There were two main reasons for adopting this approach. First, it was considered more important at this stage to know whether or not mentoring could support change in the children than to be certain that this was the cause. Positive findings would signal the need both for continuation of the project in the same form and for a randomised control trial. Secondly, the schools were reluctant, and in some cases unwilling, to allow random assignment of target children to the matched group. Although this might have been pursued further, the co-operation of the schools was essential if the project was to continue and this phase of the evaluation was to be completed satisfactorily.

In practice, the use of this design and, particularly the inclusion of a matched group of children with baseline and outcome assessments, provided crucial information. In particular, without the matched group the findings would have given a spurious impression of improvements in the children due to mentoring. The findings do not show whether both groups of children improved as a result of other interventions, simply through age, or because extreme scores tend to regress towards the mean. These issues need clarification in future studies.

For the moment, it is worth highlighting the power of a matched group design, since the comparison group inevitably adds to the cost of evaluations, which is a major concern for funding bodies. A further lesson which emerged here is the value of measures which are obtained independently of the stakeholders receiving the programme. This is not to say that the stakeholders including, importantly, the children need not be asked. Their approval and sense that progress is made are essential to the viability of any intervention. Still, they have a vested interest in the programme, while it is unrealistic to expect them to be able to separate the effects of the intervention from developments which occur as a result of age or other factors. The advantage, particularly, of norm-referenced assessments is that progress can be evaluated against a set of benchmarks, providing evidence both of the extent of change and whether the outcomes approximate normality. More measures of this kind need to be collected in future.

Lastly, the findings have reinforced Graham's [1998] argument about the need for measures of behaviour, as well as psychological change. Here, too, the point is not that psychological measures are uninformative: indeed, where programmes deliberately target changes in psychological variables, such as trust, it will be essential to measure them. Rather, the lesson is that reported psychological changes do not necessarily translate into improvements in behaviour, particularly across contexts and settings. Behaviour needs to be evaluated because it is demonstrable evidence of change. Moreover, in the crime prevention area, behaviour is the most tangible reflection we have of children's current and future problems.

The limitations of this evaluation also provide some insights. One clear shortfall was our inability to provide independent measures of the children's behaviour in their home environments, which would have allowed confirmation of the parents' and children's reports. A second is the lack of home measures from the children in the matched group and their parents, which would have indicated whether the changes reported for the mentored children at home would have occurred in the absence of mentoring. These measures are difficult to obtain for practical reasons and were beyond our resources. Obtaining them in future falls within the general challenge of developing benchmark assessments for this area.

## Project management and funding

The importance of a reliable project administrator, who takes responsibility for holding and chasing up records has already been mentioned, but is hard to over-emphasise. Much of the information needed for evaluation purposes is also needed for project management, so that this post is invaluable on both sides. It can fall by the wayside in the competition for limited funding, but in our estimation is not a post on which compromises should be made.

Secondly, it will be beneficial where possible to set up the evaluation at the same time as the project. Although there is increasing recognition of the benefits of evaluations, they are also a burden to the project, particularly if requirements such as baseline measurements are introduced after the project has found its way. Tact and sensitivity will always be needed on both sides, but an understanding from the outset of the different roles should help the project and evaluators to work towards the same end.

Finally, we would like to add our voice to others who have pointed out the inadvisability of three-year funding for projects. Even when projects are outstandingly competent and active, as in the case of CHANCE, they take a year or more to become established. With a three-year cycle, the project almost inevitably has to switch its attention to continued funding in the second or third year, with the result that it cannot sustain its main work. In effect, the funding arrangement hampers the project from achieving its purpose. In CHANCE's case, its search for funding was successful, but at a cost to its recruitment, and knock-on cost to the evaluation, which had to be lengthened because of the recruitment shortfall.

Five-year funding, coupled with stringent evaluation before projects are funded, may provide one solution. An alternative is to set up arrangements for transition funding at the outset, and to develop administrative networks which support projects in finding the support they need, so that they are able to devote as much time and energy as possible to their primary purposes.

# References

Audit Commission (1996). *Misspent Youth: Young People and Crime.* London, Audit Commission Publications.

Babinski LM Hartsough CS & Lambert NM.(1999). *Childhood conduct problems, hyperactivity, and inattention as predictors of adult criminal activity.* Journal of Child Psychology & Psychiatry, 40, 347-355.

Barclay GC & Tavares CT (1999). *Digest 4: Information on the Criminal Justice System for England & Wales.* London , Home Office Research & Statistics Directorate.

Bennett K, Lipman E, Racine Y & Offord (1998). *Annotation: do measures of externalizing behaviour in normal populations predict later outcomes?* Journal of Child Psychology & Psychiatry, 39, 1059-1070.

Buist M (2000). *Young People's Views Of The Befriending (Mentoring) Scheme Delivered by Edinburgh Volunteer Tutors Organisation.* Edinburgh, Edinburgh VTO.

Clarke A & Tarling R (1998). *Dalston Youth Project, Part B, An Evaluation; Interim Report.* London, Home Office.

Edens, JF, Cavall TA & Hughes JN (1999). *The self-systems of aggressive children: a cluster analytic investigation.* Journal of Child Psychology & Psychiatry, 40, 441-453.

Farrington, D. P. (1996). *Understanding and Preventing Youth Crime.* York Publishing Services: Joseph Rowntree Foundation.

Goodman, R. (1997). *The Strengths and Difficulties Questionnaire: a research note.* Journal of Child Psychology & Psychiatry, 38, 581-586.

Graham J & Bowling B. (1995). *Young Children and Crime.* London, Home Office.

Graham J (1998). *What works in preventing criminality.* In Goldblatt P & Lewis C (Eds) *Reducing Offending: An Assessment of Research Evidence On Ways Of Dealing With Offending Behaviour.* London; Home Office.

Grossman JB & Johnson A (1998). *Assessing the effectiveness of mentor programs.* In JB Grossman (Ed) Contemporary Issues in Mentoring. Philadelphia, Public Private Ventures.

Harter S & Pike RG (1980). *The Pictorial Scale of Perceived Competence and Acceptance for Young Children.* Denver; University of Denver.

Henrich C, Brown JA & Aber JL (1999). *Evaluating the effectiveness of school-based violence prevention: developmental approaches.* Society for Research in Child Development Social Policy Report, vol XIII no.3. SRCD, University of Michigan.

Hoza B, Waschbusch DA, Pelham WE, Molina BSG, Milich R (2000). *Attention-Deficit /HyperactivityDisordered and control boys' responses to social success and failure.* Child Development, 71, 432-446.

Ivers V. (1999). *Trans Age Action: Evaluation of Pilot Projects, 1995-1998.* London, Age Concern.

Loeber, R. (1990). *Development and risk factors of juvenile antisocial behaviour and delinquency.* Clinical Psychology Review 10:1-41.

McGill DE (1999). *Mentoring as an early intervention strategy: the experience of Big Brothers Big Sisters of America. In R Bayley (ed) Transforming Children's Lives: the Importance of Early Intervention.* London, Family Policy Studies Centre.

*Mentoring News (2000).* The Newsletter of the National Mentoring Network, Manchester.

Morton-Cooper A & Palmer A (1996). *Mentoring & Preceptorship.* Oxford, Blackwell Science.

Oliver C, Aggleton P & Rivers K. (2000). *Mentoring in Health Promotion: A Review of the Literature.* Report prepared for the Health Education Authority, UK.

Robins LN & Rutter M (1990). *Straight and devious pathways from childhood to adulthood.* Cambridge: Cambridge University Press.

Rutter M & Garmezy N (1983). *Developmental psychopathology.* In E.M. Hetherington (ed) Handbook of Child Psychology 4th Edition, Vol 4. New York, John Wiley & Sons.

Schweinhart LJ & Weikert DP (1993). *A Summary Of Significant Benefits: The High/Scope Perry Preschool Study Through Age 27.* Ypsilanti, High Scope Press.

Selekman MD (1997). *Solution-Focused Therapy with Children.* London, The Guilford Press.

St James-Roberts I & Samlal Singh C (1998). *Evaluation of Project CHANCE Islington: Phase 1 Report.* London, The Home Office.

St James-Roberts I, Sleep J, Morris S, Owen, C & Gillham P (2001) *Use of a behavioural programme in the first three months to prevent infant crying and sleeping problems.* Journal of Paediatrics & Child Health, 37, 289-297.

Tierney JP, Grossman J B, Resch NL (1995). *Making a Difference: An Impact Study of Big Brothers/Big Sisters.* Philadelphia, Public/Private Ventures.

Utting D (1996). *Reducing criminality among young people: a sample of relevant programmes in the United Kingdom.* London: Home Office.

Webster-Stratton C & Hammond M (1997). *Treating children with early onset conduct problems: a comparison of child and parent training interventions.* Journal of Consulting and Clinical Psychology, 65, 93-109.

Weissberg RP & Greenberg MT (1998). *School and community competence enhancement and prevention programs.* In IE Sigel & KA Renninger (eds) Handbook of Child Psychology, Volume 4, 5th Edition, PP 877-954. Chichester, J Wiley & Sons.

# RDS Publications

## Requests for Publications

Copies of our publications and a list of those currently available may be obtained from:

Home Office
Research, Development and Statistics Directorate
Communication Development Unit
Room 275, Home Office
50 Queen Anne's Gate
London SW1H 9AT
Telephone: 020 7273 2084 (answerphone outside of office hours)
Facsimile: 020 7222 0211
E-mail: publications.rds@homeoffice.gsi.gov.uk

alternatively

why not visit the RDS website at

Internet: http://www.homeoffice.gov.uk/rds/index.html

where many of our publications are available to be read on screen or downloaded for printing.